inside story

creative writing for students

SUE LAWSON & JODI TOERING

For Bruce,
my favourite wordsmith. S.L.

For Bambi Afford,
who always has time for a story. J.T.

First published in 2024 by

wdog.com.au

Melbourne, Australia

Designed by Guy Holt 2024

ISBN: 9781742036670 (hbk)

Printed and bound by Everbest Ltd

10 9 8 7 6 5 4 3 2 1 24 25 26 27 28 29

Contents

Making a Start

Inside Story is full of writing ideas and exercises to help build your understanding of writing.

This book is a bit like the writing process. You don't have to write from the beginning of your story, and you don't have to begin *Inside Story* on page one. If you're interested in characters, start there. If you'd like to work on your description and detail, focus on that chapter first.

Experiment!
Work through the book backwards if you like. But most of all, enjoy discovering what makes a great story.

Tools

When you boil it down, writers need only three things – their imagination, something to write with, and something to write on.

You don't need an expensive computer or fancy notebooks to be a writer. You can write anywhere – at the kitchen table or at the beach. Pretty pens, laptops and journals might be fun to use, but they don't make your writing better. Only practice does that.

Writers' Notebooks

Writers are collectors. They gather quotes, headlines, snippets of conversations, descriptions of places and photographs. Many writers keep these bits and pieces in a notebook. They do this so they remember what they've observed. All those notes and ideas gathered in a notebook might later spark a story idea or help describe a scene.

Try keeping your own notebook. When you see or hear something that interests you, write it in your notebook. Spotted a cartoon, photo or headline that appeals to you? Add that to your notebook too.

We all think we will remember things later, but the truth is that we often forget. Notebooks help us capture our thoughts and ideas for later.

The problem

Good writing captures the reader's attention, right until the very last word. Writers use many techniques to keep readers turning pages. Some of these are setting, plot, characters and dialogue. But none of these will work well if the story doesn't have an interesting problem.

A story's problem is vital. It's like a road map. The beginning of the story introduces the problem. The middle works towards finding a solution. Once the problem is solved, the story is over.

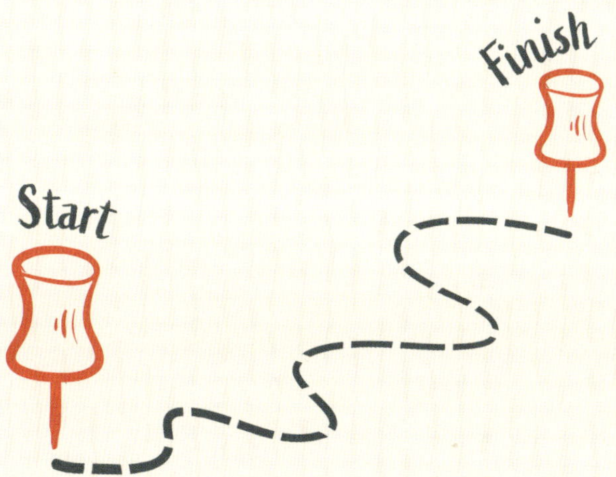

Warm-ups

Just as stretching prepares your body for physical activity, writing warm-ups prepare your brain for creative writing. Writing warm-ups are messy and jumbled, but that is how they are supposed to be.

What you write doesn't matter, just write! Write about your bedroom, your favourite food or the feel of grass under your toes. We've added prompts you might like to use, too. Don't panic if you go off topic. Keep writing.

If you can, use a pen and paper for your warm-ups rather than a computer. There's nothing like writing by hand to free up your imagination.

How to do a writing warm-up

Preparation for writing warm-ups is easy. You will need a pen and paper, your writer's notebook and a timer. You can use a phone timer, a clock or even the oven timer.

Now you're ready:

1. Pick a topic, make up your own or use one suggested in this book.
2. Set the timer. Start with two minutes. As you become more confident with warm-ups, set the timer for longer.
3. Write! Forget about spelling. Forget about being neat. Just write.
4. Don't stop.
5. When the timer goes off, you're done!

You might never return to what you write in a warm-up, and that's okay. However, it is a good idea to keep your warm-ups. You might use all or part of a warm-up in a story one day.

Warm-up prompts

- If you could spend an hour with someone famous, who would it be and why?
- Invent five new uses for a pram.
- What would your superpower be?
- What is your favourite day of the week? Why?
- Imagine you are the first human to see an elephant. Describe it.
- Plan a surprise party for a garden gnome.
- Write a 'to-do' list for a pirate.
- You find a battered old suitcase. What is inside?
- Pretend you are a cat. Write a diary entry about your day.
- Imagine you find a secret door in your wardrobe. Where does it lead?
- You are locked in a shopping centre after hours. What happens?

- The lift you are in shudders to a stop. What happens next?
- Write about the best place you have visited.
- Imagine you are a flea living on a dog. Describe your home.
- A meteor falls to Earth and cracks open. What is inside?
- Write a letter to a fairytale character.
- If your favourite toy could talk, what would it say?
- If you could go anywhere, where would you go?
- What is the scariest place you've ever been?
- Describe your ideal bedroom.
- Brainstorm the colour 'red'. What comes to mind? Try other colours.
- A bird lands on your windowsill. What does it say to you?

Write on from...

- I opened the can of dog food and out jumped ...
- Right now, I am feeling ...
- My grandfather used to collect ...
- Instead of being bright and golden, the sun was ...
- She slipped her hand into her pocket and felt ...
- It looked like blueberries and ice-cream, but it tasted like ...
- My life was boring until ...
- No one expects to find a whale in their ...
- It looked like a feather, but it was a ...
- Sure, she was a strange old lady, but no one expected her to ...

Memories

Write about:

- The last time you laughed until your stomach hurt.
- Your earliest memory.
- The worst thing you've ever tasted.
- Your best friend at kindergarten.
- A time you were caught in the rain.
- Your first pet.
- The first book you remember reading or being read to you.
- The most boring job you've had to do at home.
- The best practical joke you've played or had played on you.
- The silliest thing you have ever seen.
- An emotion:

anger, surprise,
trust, guilt, sadness,
boredom, love, fear, joy.

Writing your story

There are four main steps in story writing:

Ideas

It can be difficult to come up with a story idea. Even published authors have days when they have run out of ideas. Luckily, when you have one of those days, there are things you can do to help.

First up, revisit your notebook and your writing warm-ups. There may be something you could develop into a story.

If you're still coming up with nothing, try the following techniques.

Brainstorming

Have you ever tried brainstorming to help you come up with a story idea? To brainstorm, pick a topic or an object. Set your timer for between five and ten minutes, then write everything that topic makes you think of. Don't censor your thoughts; just write them down. If you hit a wall and can't think of more, keep trying. The best ideas often come at the end of a brainstorming session.

When the timer goes off, examine your list. Pick a few words that stand out.

Now it's time to ask questions to develop those ideas. The best question is 'what if?'.

What if?

'What if?' is story magic. It unlocks your imagination and encourages your mind to be inquisitive.

You can use 'what if' with your brainstorm words. You can even 'what if?' an object. In fact, 'what if?' works with just about anything.

To use 'what if?', pick an object, word or picture. Ask yourself 'what if?', and let your imagination run wild. Keep going until you have an idea that excites you.

Here are a few examples to try:

What if ...

- your cat started talking?
- you became a character in the book you are reading?
- you could breathe underwater?
- your arms turned to rubber?

Pay attention

Writers are observant. They can create an entire story from something they see.

Keep your eyes and ears open. Notice how somebody pushes a supermarket trolley. Listen to snippets of conversations. Read street signs and advertising banners. Examine graffiti.

Throw in a 'what if?' and see what you come up with.

Websites, newspapers and magazines

News websites, newspapers and magazines are great sources for story ideas. Pay attention to headlines, advertisements, images and articles.

Characters

Another way to come up with a story idea is to create a character. Once you know that character well, build a story around them. More about characters later.

Objects

The magic question 'what if?' and any object will spark ideas.

Try pairing these objects with 'what if?':

- An autograph
- Feathers
- An old cotton reel
- Sunglasses
- A piece of jewellery
- A rock
- A chocolate wrapper
- A movie ticket

Your own experiences

Your life can be a source of story ideas. You don't have to retell your experiences exactly as they happened. This is called a recount. To make your memories and experiences a fictional narrative, change details, add new characters, leave bits out and exaggerate.

Planning your story

Planning your story helps you organise your ideas before you start to write. There are many ways to plan. Try a few to find what works best for you.

The problem

Just knowing your story problem is planning. Remember, the problem gives you the story's beginning, middle and end.

Before you start writing your draft, write down your problem:

- My story problem is ...
- Write it in your notebook or stick it on a pinboard where you write — having it on display will help you keep your story on track.
- If you feel stuck while writing, return to the story problem and check that you are focused on solving it.

Remember: Plans are not set in stone. They are just outlines that grow and change as you write.

Story arc

Another way to plan your story is to use a story arc. Draw a rainbow shape on your page and write 'problem' on the left and 'solution' on the right. Then, on the rainbow, add details and events that you want to include in your story.

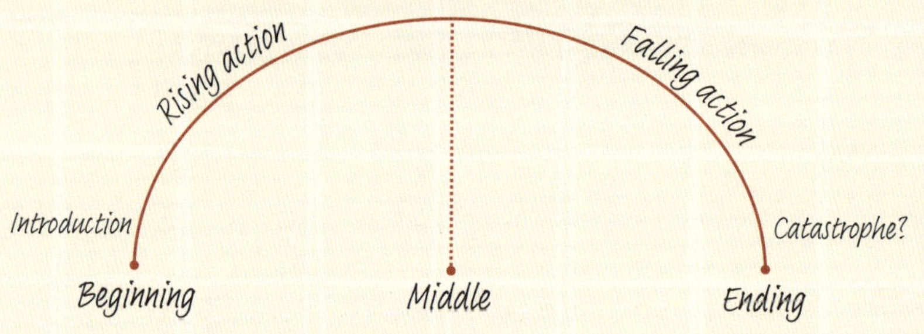

Mind mapping

Mind maps help you gather your ideas in one place. They are a fast way to plan a story. When using mind maps as a story plan, add words, sentences and, if you like, drawings to capture your ideas. Once you have the main points on paper, you can add more detail and order your thoughts.

Mind maps are messy, and that's fine. Writing is a messy business.

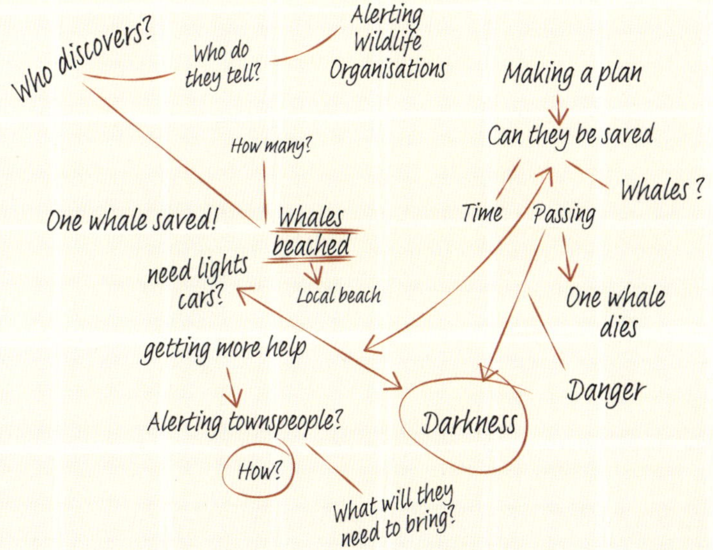

Drafting a story

Just as you can't make a clay pot until you have a lump of clay, you can't write a great story until you have a draft.

Drafts are the beginning. They are never the final story. Every good writer writes and rewrites their work to make it the best it can be.

When drafting a story, your focus is on the story itself. That's why it's normal for drafts to have spelling mistakes, dull words and grammar problems. A first draft will often have chunks of information missing and can be out of order.

While writing your draft, keep reminding yourself: 'Write the draft, fix it later.'

You can fix anything when you have a draft to edit. You can't edit a blank page!

Drafting Tip:
If you're using lined paper to write your draft, write on every second line. This gives you space to edit later.

Titles

Titles are important. A good title grabs a reader's attention. However, you don't need a title before you start writing.

While you are drafting, you can call your story anything – *Monday's Story*, *Story About a Dog* – it doesn't matter. Once you've written your draft and know what your story is about, then you can find the perfect title.

Remember:
Titles are important, but they aren't the first thing you need to write.

Where to begin

When it comes to drafts, you don't need to start at the beginning of your story. You can start at the end, or with a scene in the middle of your story. Start anywhere.

When you've finished your draft, it's time to look critically at how you start the story. We will come back to later.

Point of view

Point of view describes how a writer chooses to tell a story. There are three points of view: first person, second person and third person.

When you're writing a draft you may switch point of view without realising. That's okay!

First person

In first person, one character, usually the main character, tells the story. The writer can only include information that this character knows and can't include anything other characters are thinking or feeling. First person allows the writer to be inside the main character's head.

First person uses pronouns such as I, me and mine.

Example: 'I opened my door and stepped outside.'

Second person

Second person asks the reader to imagine they are part of the story. Second person point of view speaks directly to the reader, and is not used often in fiction. Second person pronouns include you, your and yours.

Example: 'You opened your door and stepped outside.'

Third person

A third person story is told as if someone is watching what is happening. This point of view is flexible and allows the writer to show the reader what many characters are feeling and thinking. Third person pronouns are he/his, she/hers, they/theirs.

Example: 'Jerry opened his door and stepped outside.'

It's up to you which point of view you choose. If you want to focus on one character, first person might be your choice. However, if you have three characters and want to share their ideas and feelings, choose third person point of view.

If you're looking for somewhere to start, try rewriting these short pieces in differing points of view:

- The cold air caught in my throat. I tried not to cough. Any sound, any tiny movement, would give away my position for sure.
- Sammy slipped down the hillside towards his crumpled grandfather.
  'Stop mucking around, Gramps,' called Sammy.
  'Stand up.' But Gramps didn't move.
- You tiptoed closer. A wedge of yellow light spilled across your feet. The mumble of your parents' voices became clearer. 'He won't like it,' your mother said with a sigh.

Beginnings

How and where you begin your story is important. A good story beginning introduces your main characters and the story's problem. A good opening should be interesting and make the reader want to keep reading.

There are many ways to create a start that hooks your reader, and most of them involve introducing your character and the problem they face as soon as you can.

Before we look at what makes a great start, remember, you polish your start after you've written your first draft.

Tip:
Name your main characters as soon as you can. This helps your reader connect with them faster.

Dialogue

Dialogue is a great way to begin a story. It introduces the reader to the problem, the characters and the setting:

> **'We can't go in there,' said Sarah, her hands trembling. 'Everyone knows that house belongs to a witch.'**
>
> **'Jackson, get off that computer right now!'**
>
> **'Izzie,' bellowed Mum, 'the dog has escaped from the yard. Again.'**

Thoughts

A character's thoughts can also introduce your character and the story problem:

> **I glanced at my watch. What was keeping Mum? She was usually the first parent at pick-up.**
>
> **Life was easy when we lived in Cannington. I knew people, and people knew me. But here, it's different. And not good different.**
>
> **Why do I always have to look after my little brothers?**

Ultimatum – do it or else

There's nothing like an ultimatum to start a story with a bang. An ultimatum not only introduces the character and the problem, it also creates a sense of urgency:

> **'You have until noon, then the dog gets it.'**
>
> **'If that room isn't tidy by the time I get back from the supermarket, there's no footy final tomorrow.'**

Action

Another good way to start a story with a bang is with action:

> **'Rayan peered over the edge of the cliff.'**
>
> **'Edi took a slow deep breath before stepping onto the stage.'**
>
> **'Aki threw his school bag onto his unmade bed.'**

The problem

Okay, we've said it before, but it's really important. The problem is like a story road map. When you know the story problem, you know where to start, what to write and when to stop writing. Start close to the problem.

You can sprinkle in backstory and details as you continue to write.

Spend time exploring novels. Read the first page of a book and see if you can name the characters, the setting and the problem by the end of the first page. Keep a record of beginnings you love in your writer's notebook.

Try writing the first sentence or two of these story problems:

- Robbie's parents have split up and he's moved with his mum to a country town called Willington. It's his first day at school.
- Jazz must swim against her former best friend, Azira, in the district freestyle championships. Jazz and Azira fought five months ago and haven't spoken since.
- Rishi has lost his brother Arjum's rare football cards.
- Duy lets Chim, his grandfather's beloved canary, out of its cage. Chim has made it outside to the clothesline.

Characters

Readers connect to stories through characters. Authors work hard to create interesting, believable characters that the reader will care about. Creating characters takes a little time, but it's worth the effort. And it's fun!

When you create a character, remember that their personality and how they behave are more important than their appearance.

Names

Character names are important. A good name suits the character's personality and the time the story is set. It can even hint at their personality. It's always best to choose fresh names rather than using your friends' or family members' names.

Create a 'character name page' in your writer's notebook. That way you always have interesting names on hand.

Try using these names to create your own character:

- Katie Steele
- Asahi Takahashi
- Aleena de Silva
- Albert Higginsworth
- Ztraer
- Mirri Hunter

How you choose to use a name can make a difference. A character called Charlie can be very different from one who insists on being called Charles.

Try creating different characters from these names:

- How is Jessie Perera different from Jessica Perera?
- How is Albert Hope different from Alby Hope?

Now try creating a name that suits these characters:

- A strong, feisty character terrified of water.
- A character who lives on a goat farm, but hates being outside.
- A ballet dancer who loves rock music and ice-cream.
- A vet who specialises in small animals.

Creating characters

You might like to create a section in your notebook that includes character profiles, pictures from magazines or other snippets of detail. It also helps to create a list of names. Remember to mix them up so you have a good representation of names.

Character profile

Just like real people, every story character has a unique personality. One way to create a believable character is to create a character profile. Character profiles help you get to know your character well. When you know your characters well, your characters come to life and it's easier to write about them.

When building a character profile, be as specific as possible. Don't say your character likes chocolate; name the chocolate. Instead of writing that they like sport, name that sport. This will give you a clearer picture of who they are.

Remember to avoid stereotypes. If you do need a grumpy man with a walking stick, make him love romantic movies and cats. Everybody, even a story character, can have a surprising side to their personality.

Use the form on the next page to help you create a character profile. Feel free to add more headings to your profile to further flesh out your character:

Character Profile

Name: ....

Age: ....

Home *(where they live)*: ....

....

Family: ....

Pets: ....

School: ....

Appearance: ....

Job/s *(can be around home or a part-time job)*: ....

....

Likes: ....

Dislikes: ....

Problems: ....

....

....

....

Character problems

You can use your character profile to think of a story idea. Look closely at the character's profile, especially their likes and dislikes. Here, you will find a problem you can develop into a story.

For example:

Alf is in his late 70s. He hates children and loves peace and quiet. His problem could be that a childcare centre is being built beside his home.

Ten-year-old Zee loves playing football. Her problem might be that she's injured her knee right before the finals.

Characters from objects and belongings:

In life, people's belongings and clothing provide information about their personality and interests. It's the same with story characters. Writers often use objects such as books, photos or jewellery to reveal information about their characters. For example, a boy who has a jar filled with feathers and books about bird breeds on his bedside table shows that he is interested in birds.

Show character by listing what's on or in your character's:

wardrobe	schoolbag	handbag
pencil case	fridge	bedside table

Dialogue

Dialogue is a balancing act between words and action. It's different from the everyday conversations you might have. In real conversations, people often don't finish sentences. They talk over each other, pull faces and use body language. In stories, every piece of dialogue has a job.

Good dialogue:

- Brings characters to life.
- Shows characters' personality and feelings.
- Shows relationships between characters.
- Provides information and details related to the story problem.
- Adds tension or drama.

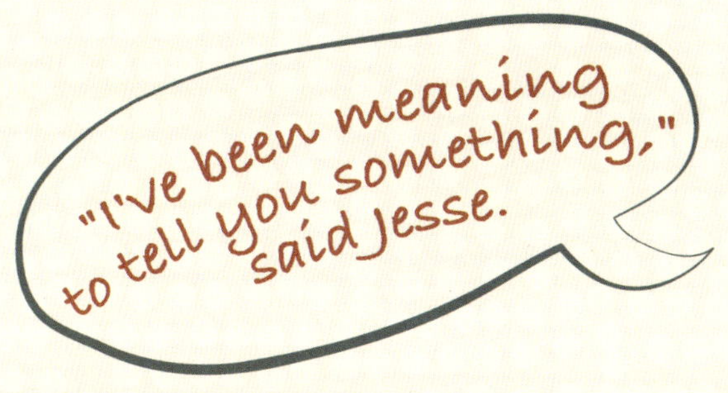

Setting out

You probably know that dialogue has its own punctuation, but there is another rule about writing dialogue that many young writers don't know. Every time a character speaks, start a new line.

Here's an example:

'Did you remember chocolate topping, Dad?' asked Lei, peering into the shopping bags.

'I did, if it was on the list,' said Dad.

'What list?'

Dad sighed. 'Lei, I told you. The list was on the fridge. I knew you weren't listening. Again.'

When writing dialogue, remember:

- Dialogue begins and ends with quotation or talking marks.
- Use attributes, for example, 'said', to show who is speaking. There are many attribute options, but writers often stick to 'said', as it doesn't distract from the story.
- Remember to add actions to your dialogue, but be careful not to go overboard.
- Each time a different character speaks, start a new line.

Try these:

- Write a short piece of dialogue between a bully and a timid person.
- Write a conversation between characters from different fairytales. For example, Cinderella and Papa Bear, or Goldilocks and the Gingerbread Man.
- Write a conversation between a child and parent that begins: 'You will go in there and apologise right now!'
- Write a conversation between an old family pet and a new one.

Dialogue activities to try with your characters:

- Your character is in a bad mood but doesn't want a friend to know why. Write a conversation between them on a bus.
- Your character is lost. Write how they would ask a stranger for directions.
- Write a conversation that starts with your character's brother saying: 'I am telling Dad.'
- Your character is worried about their best friend. They're out walking. What does your character say?

Remember:
Dialogue shows character
and adds to the story.

Setting

Where and when you set your story is important. The setting helps set up the problem, adds mood to your writing and adds to the narrative.

Set your story wherever you like. On a deserted beach. Inside a haunted house. Under a caravan. Deep inside a cave.

Set your story in any time or era you choose. The present. The year 1675. Twenty years in the future.

The trick is to make sure the setting suits your story.

Choosing a setting

The story problem will help you decide the best setting for your story. There's no point in setting a story on the moon if the story problem is that the character can't make friends at school. While writing, keep in mind the time period in which the story takes place. If the story is set in the 1930s, for example, you can't have your characters answering a mobile phone or checking Google.

It can help to revisit your favourite books. Think about where the story was set and its role in the story. Ask yourself if the story would still work if it was set somewhere else.

Creating the setting

Just as you need to know your characters well, you need to know your setting. Draw a map of the town or a plan of the character's house. If you set your story somewhere you haven't been, spend time researching that area so you know what it's like.

Use these examples to experiment with setting:

- Write a paragraph describing a setting you know well — your classroom, bedroom, backyard or family car.
- Pick a character from a picture book or fairytale and place them in a different story setting (e.g. write about Cinderella in the little pigs' house).
- Describe a zoo from the point of view of an animal.
- Create a setting for a character who is timid and quiet.
- Imagine that one of your characters is scared. See if you can show emotion through the setting. Experiment with other emotions.

Revising and Editing Your Story

Once you have written your first draft, it's time to edit. Editing is just as important as writing. In fact, some writers believe editing is even more important. Editing is where you make your story shine.

Many writers use the term 'editing' to cover all aspects of redrafting their work. However, there are two parts to redrafting. One is called revising, the other is editing. When redrafting your work, focus on one area at a time.

Revising

When writers revise their work, they focus on the big picture – the story. This is where you might add extra descriptions, delete sentences or reorder scenes. You might even decide to change the point of view. Think of revising as the time when you make big changes to the story.

Revise your story first. Once you are happy with the shape of your story, turn your attention to editing, including spelling, punctuation and grammar.

When revising and editing your writing, always read your work aloud. If you stumble or if a word pulls you up, pay attention. This is often an area that needs to change.

Questions to ask while revising your work:

- Does the beginning grab the reader?
- Have I named my characters early in the story?
- Are the characters real and believable?
- Have I described the setting and characters well?
- Have I avoided stereotypes?
- Is there too much/too little dialogue?
- When my character speaks, does the dialogue move the story forward?
- Is my character waffling?
- Have I repeated myself?
- Does the action flow and build to the climax?
- Does each part of the story make sense?
- Do I need to change the order of events?
- Do I need to add or delete information?
- Is my ending satisfying?

About tense

Tense is the word used to describe the time an action occurs.

There are three types of tense:

1. Past tense, where something has happened:
   'Steve walked to the game.'

2. Present tense, meaning the action is occurring now:
   'Steve is walking to the game.'

3. Future tense, an action that is going to happen:
   'Steve will walk to the game.'

While you're drafting your story you might slip from one tense into another. That's perfectly normal. When you're editing, choose the tense you think suits your story and stick to that. Tense must be consistent.

Editing

When writers edit, they examine the fine details of their writing. This means that they look for spelling, punctuation and grammar problems, as well as checking tense and word choice.

Think of editing as getting into the nitty gritty of your story:

- Read your work aloud. Pay attention to where you stumble.
- Drafts are messy! Write on your draft, cross out words, draw arrows, add labels. Do whatever works for you.
- When you are concentrating on choosing stronger words, be wary of searching the thesaurus. Bigger words aren't always better.
- Once you finish your draft, put it away for a few days or a week before you begin editing. The break helps you see your story with fresh eyes.
- Kill lazy words — got, lots, then, so, but, nice, some, beautiful — and replace them with stronger ones.

Finally, if you have written your story on a computer, it can be useful to print out a copy to edit. You might find you edit better when working on a hard copy.

Questions to ask while editing:

- Are there enough details for the reader to see a clear picture?
- Are there too many boring details?
- Do you have unnecessary information?
- Can you use a stronger noun or verb to create a better description?

Description and detail

A story is a bit like a dinosaur skeleton. The idea or plot is the bare bones. The description and detail are the muscle and skin that give the dinosaur its unique appearance.

When you are revising, pay attention to your detail and description. Do you have the right balance? Too much will slow down your story. Not enough makes it difficult for the reader to know what is happening.

Choosing words

When writing a draft, writers focus on the story. They don't pay attention to choosing great words and spelling them correctly. Editing is the time to pay attention to vocabulary.

As you revise, look for weak words and swap them for ones that paint clear mind pictures. That doesn't mean you have to go nuts with big words. Make sure your language and description suit the story.

Show, don't tell

Writers love the expression 'show don't tell'. But what does it mean? It's simple: instead of telling the reader how a character feels or what is going on, the author shows them. Showing makes stories more interesting.

A sentence like, 'She was angry', tells the reader how the character feels.

On the other hand, 'Get out,' she yelled, slamming her fist on the table', uses dialogue and action to show how the character feels.

Can you pick which one of these sentences is show and which is tell?

'The room was untidy.'

'Crumpled socks and shirts covered the floor rug.'

Be specific

Another way to 'show, don't tell' is to be specific in your descriptions. Rich description doesn't always need adjectives and adverbs. Choosing stronger nouns and verbs paints a much clearer picture. Name objects and places where you can, and watch out for adverbs. For example, 'He ran quickly' is much stronger when changed to 'He sprinted.' The use of the word 'sprinted' adds more urgency to the sentence.

When you do this, your sentences and imagery are clearer:

'The big, black dog blocked the footpath.'

This is an okay sentence, but it doesn't create a clear mind picture. What if we chose a stronger noun?

'The Rottweiler blocked the footpath.'

'A Labrador puppy sat in the middle of the footpath.'

Can you see the difference? A stronger noun creates a much clearer picture.

When writing, try to name everything. This includes characters, dog breeds, types of trees and plants, colours or car brands.

Try rewriting these sentences using 'show, don't tell' and more specific language:

- The boy ate his dinner.
- The girl went to the beach.
- She sat on a seat.
- The dog was sad.
- It was dark.
- I was hot.
- I am cold.
- The man was angry.
- The room was empty.
- I had fun at the circus.

Now try showing character in these sentences. Replace the dull nouns with specific nouns.

Example:

'He ate something.'
'Ayaan ate a Granny Smith apple.'

Your turn:

- Mel parked the car.
- Jerri loved sport.
- Angie gave her grandparents flowers.
- Corey closed her book.
- Sameer dropped his bag.
- The lion ate meat.
- Darby caught a fish.
- He picked flowers for his mum.

Waffly words

Writers use words to paint vivid pictures. Waffly words and phrases like 'sort of', 'kind of', 'some' and 'very' make for a less vivid picture. Look at how using a different word changes the imagery in these sentences:

> **'I ate some chocolate.'**
>
> **'I ate a family-size block of chocolate.'**
>
> **'I ate a Lindt Chocolate Ball.'**
>
> **'Stacey was fairly tall, with rather longish, messy looking hair.'**
>
> **'Stacey was tall, with long, messy hair.'**

Experiment with changing these dull sentences to show meaning and create clearer imagery:

- It was a pretty long wait.
- She ate the biscuit.
- He drew some pictures.
- She ate some fruit.
- He bought some nuts.
- The house was falling down.
- The building was abandoned.
- The sea was rough.
- The mountain was high.
- The party was exciting.
- I had fun at the circus.

Adjectives and adverbs

Simple writing is powerful and creates clear mind pictures. When you are editing, remember that less is more. One strong adjective is much better than a long list of words.

For example:

> **'He pulled the crumpled, blue, striped flannelette sheets over his head.'**
>
> **'He pulled the crumpled sheets over his head.'**

Many authors don't like to use adverbs.
Do you know why?

It is because it's better to choose a stronger verb than to add an adverb.

For example:

> **'He walked quickly.'**
> **'He ran.'**
>
> **'She said angrily.'**
> **'She yelled.'**

Have a go at rewriting these examples:

- He shut the door noisily.
- She spoke loudly.
- He walked slowly.
- She played nicely.
- He crossed the road safely.

In your writer's notebook, experiment with replacing adverbs with strong verbs.

Description and detail ideas

- Choose an image, perhaps an online photo or one you've taken. Use unexpected ways to describe the image.
- Write a paragraph describing an everyday object to someone who has never seen one.
- Use your senses to describe your favourite place. You have five senses. Don't rely solely on sight and sound.
- Go back to an older piece of your writing. Circle any nouns and verbs. Try to replace them with stronger words.

Remember:
Add detail and description when you are revising and editing your work.

Painting word pictures

Artists use pencils and paintbrushes to create images. Authors use words and language. Figurative language is another method authors use to paint word pictures. Figurative language compares objects, people – anything – in unlikely ways.

There are many kinds of figurative language:

Simile: compares two things.
'Jack was as hot as fire.'

Metaphor: a describing word or phrase which isn't literally true.
'Jack was burning up.'

Personification: giving an object human characteristics or actions.
'The fire shrieked through the trees.'

Idiom: words or phrases that aren't meant to be taken literally.
'It's raining cats and dogs.'

Onomatopoeia: a word that sounds like what it is describing.
'Splash', 'Thunk', 'Whoosh'.

Hyperbole: exaggerated or over-the-top descriptions.
'My schoolbag weighs a tonne.'

Alliteration: words that start with the same sound or letter.
'Five fat flying frogs.'

Personification:

- Write a list of nouns. Now give your nouns human actions or characteristics. For example: Waves – whisper, sigh, shriek, growl.
- Create two lists, one of everyday objects and the other of human actions.
- Pick a word from each list and put them in a sentence. For example: 'The desk groaned under the weight of his books.'

Onomatopoeia:

- List nouns in one column and onomatopoeia in another column.
- Now mix up the words from the two columns to create new combinations. Some will work, others won't, and that's okay. For example, we think this one works: 'The damaged spaceship gurgled through the atmosphere.'

Exaggeration:

- Use exaggeration to describe yourself, family, celebrities, athletes or friends. For example: 'My brother is as loud as a jet engine.'

Alliteration:

- Choose an animal. Write as many sentences as you can using words that begin with the same letter as the animal. For example: 'Anteaters are accomplished anglers.'
- Try plants, sports, furniture, stationery – anything you can think of!

General ideas:

- Write about a character who is underwater. What would they do, see, feel, hear? Experiment with the five senses.
- Imagine a character who is eating something they hate. Use figurative language to describe what they are feeling and tasting.
- Write a sensory poem about colours or feelings, or both.

A word about clichés

Clichés are overused words or phrases. Clichés are another example of figurative language, and they have their place. However, in creative writing it's better to create new and fresh imagery.

Examples:

'Better late than never.'

'I have a frog in my throat.'

'Black as coal.'

Have a go at rewriting these clichés to create fresh images:

Similes

- Brave as a lion
- As clean as a whistle
- They fight like cats and dogs
- Cute as a button
- Cold as ice
- Tough as nails

Metaphors

- Life is a rollercoaster
- His room is a disaster
- Her voice could shatter glass
- It broke my heart
- Icing on the cake

Idioms

- It cost an arm and a leg
- Piece of cake
- Easy as ABC
- Let's call it a day
- She's in hot water
- We're all in the same boat

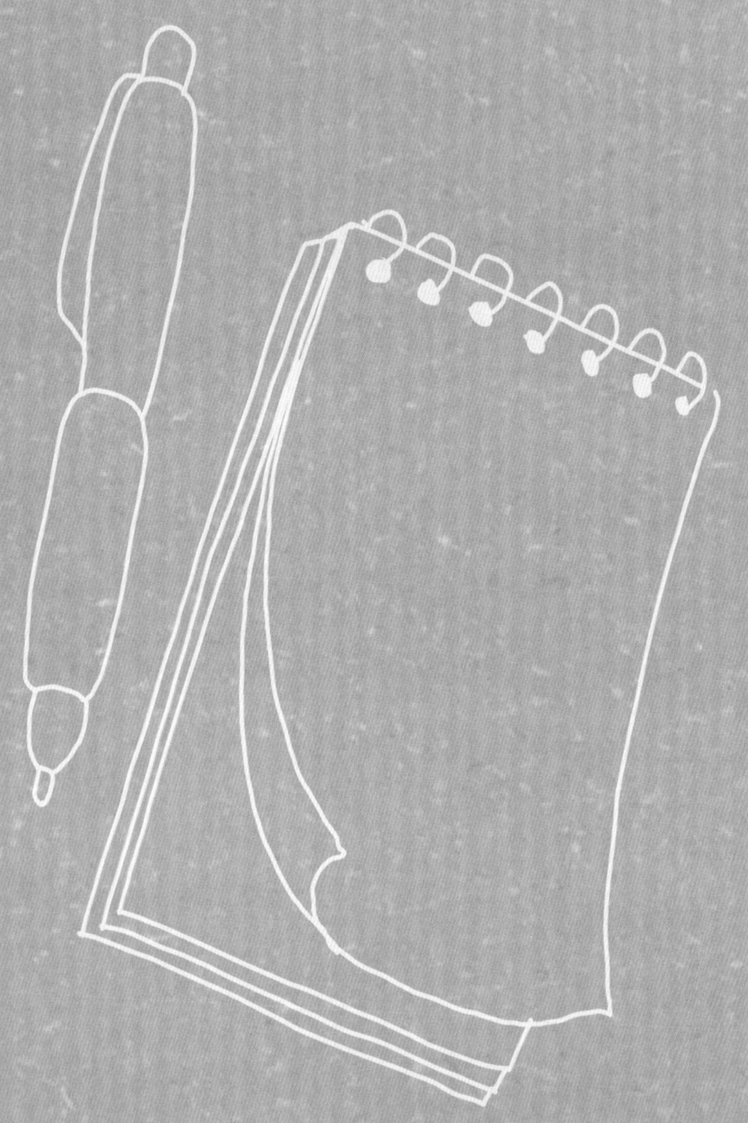

What NOW?

Once you have finished editing, your story is done. What you do with your story now is up to you. You might like to share it with friends, or perhaps you'd like to illustrate your story and print it yourself. You might be ready to start a new project. Whatever you choose, make sure you celebrate.

Writing a story takes hard work and commitment.

Congratulations!

Perhaps you'd like to be a published writer? Well, you are now well on your way to making that happen. Becoming a writer takes hard work and persistence. Most of all, you need to keep practising and building your skill. Practise, practise and then practise some more.

Our advice to you is to keep writing. Try writing different styles. Have a go at writing short stories, reports, action pieces and poems. Write a play. Write letters. Keep a writer's notebook. Experiment with genre and point of view.

And finally, read! The more you read, in all genres, the more you will learn about writing.

Good luck. We hope writing brings you as much joy as it brings us.

Glossary

adjective: a word that describes a noun

adverb: a word that describes a verb

alliteration: words that begin with the same sound or letter

blurb: a short description of a book, written to capture a reader's interest

character: a person in a narrative

cliché: commonly used descriptive phrases

dialogue: characters speaking in a narrative

first person: when a story is told by the main character

imagery: using words to paint mind pictures for the reader

metaphor: describing an object or person by comparing it with something else

narrator: the character telling the story

narrative: a story; fiction

noun: a naming word

plot: the events that occur in a story

point of view: the perspective from which a writer tells a story

second person: a point of view which uses 'you'

setting: where the story takes place

simile: compares one object with another; it often has the word 'like' in it

third person: a story told by a narrator who can see everything that is happening

verb: an action word

Notes